flF419417

To God, thanks for everything! - P.S.

To all new parents and their family pets. Special thanks to Kelle Straw, who let me paint her Italian Greyhounds! - M.E.

NEW MOM, NEW DAD
A BEDTIME RHYME

Penny Shire  Illustrated by Maureen Engle

It's **bedtime** new mom, new dad.

Visit **bath** and changing pad.

Put her down with a prayer and a **kiss**.

A **whimper** signals what's amiss.

Her **pacifier's** fallen out.

Put it back before she shouts!

Tip-toe out, close the door.

It hasn't been **five minutes** more...

Before the baby starts to **cry**.
"I'll get it," mom says with a sigh.

Another feeding, laid down again. Baby **dreaming**, all good when...

Mom sits up. She's heard a **sound**.

It's dad's turn to do a round.

He **rocks** her till eyes start to droop. It's going well until...

she **poops**!

Once the diaper comes undone, she sprays him with a **number one**!

He finally completes the change. Eyes are red, hair deranged.

He **flops** back down upon the bed. Body tired, brain is dead.

She starts to moan.
They drag their feet.

Then she **gasps**!

Hearts' skip a beat.

Footsteps **running** down the hall!

Hurry now no time to stall!

Swept up in arms, a **vomit** soars.

Alive, **thank God**! Now back to snores.

They go to bed but still awake,
listening for each breath she takes.

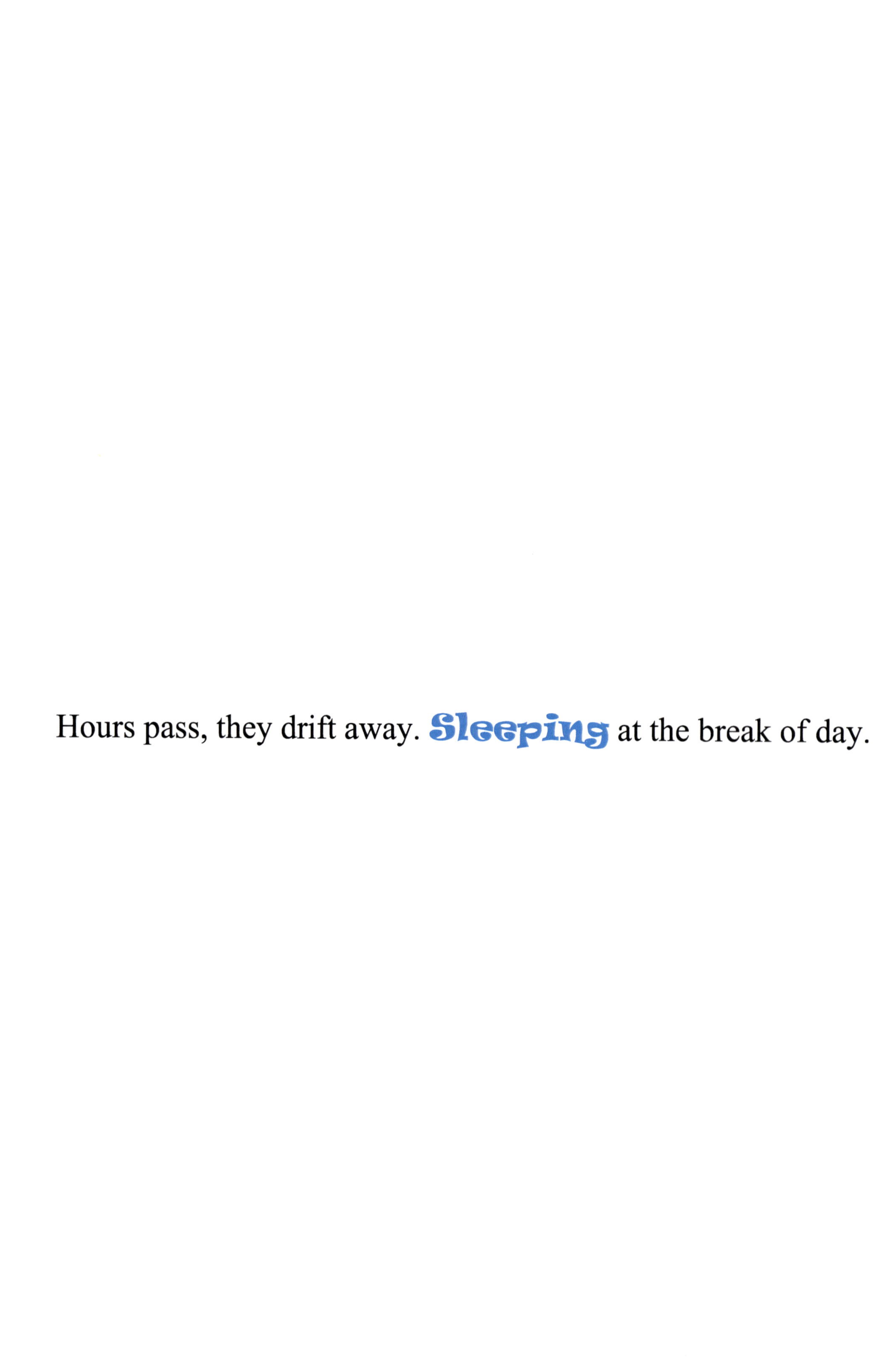

Hours pass, they drift away. **Sleeping** at the break of day.

The End...

Till tomorrow
night.